The tide breathes out

new work by Lemon Tree Writers

Published in 2006 by **Lemon Tree Writers**
5 West North Street, Aberdeen AB24 5AT

ISBN: 0-9553086-1-5 / 978-0-9553086-1-1

Lemon Tree Writers

Lemon Tree Writers were established in 1992 and meet regularly in Aberdeen to share and discuss writing of all kinds. The group's members are writers, published and unpublished, from all over the North East and in addition to the regular meetings many have participated in workshops, retreats, drama productions, readings and broadcasts. In 2005 four members of the group published "Spinners and Spoons", a Koo Press chapbook, and "Meeting Points" showcasing the work of four more writers from the group, was launched at the Word Festival in 2006. We hope in this anthology to give you a fuller flavour of our work.

Lemon Tree Writers acknowledge the support of the Lemon Tree and of Aberdeen City Council.

www.lemontree.org

ABERDEEN
CITY COUNCIL

Contents

Tasmania

And in the frame: a peacock's tail
strutting and uncontained
plumed spilling beyond
the frame to mesmerize.
And here is the peacock
all blue plume and cobra neck
crooked and jutting
a stalker with indian jewel eyes
guileless and yet still as a dancer.
And on the hill above a lake
your eyeless figure.
I barely remember the lake
with bleeding margins of timber
a temperate forest
and a stone path
up which you lead me blindfold
a twisting purposeless path
up which you lead
and I follow.

March 29 2005

REBECCA JONES

Floorboards

Choose your floorboards carefully.
If you are going to have an affair

you'll remember to wash your collars
but you'll forget about the hair

that will drift down from her head
as she lies guileless under your skin

bare on the futon on the floor
the silent polished boards all revealing.

For years I was told I imagined it
but now it's me that's drugged with regret.

So in future, darling, remember that jarrah is a dark wood
and is far better suited to a brunette.

To have bedded a blonde on jarrah
was an oversight of your cunning plan.

Your blonde should have been shagged on lighter wood -
pine, laminate or even linoleum.

As for us redheads, may I advise simply
that you invest in expensive polished cherry

but next time just clean under the bed
and if you made this your priority

there would be no harsh words or acrimony
and as for drugs or accusations, neither of us will need to
worry about any.

January 2005

Decomposition II

On the table, on his side of the bed,
his alarm clock with its yellow bell
shaded from that singular hell -
the slap and fumble - the morning shock,
silently collecting layers of household dust
bed-blown chaff of lovers bagged and lost.
Under that yellow bell, it drifts like varve clay
slough from the vigour of clandestine foreplay
the crust of a kiss, the rub of a thigh,
a lash perhaps, from the wipe of an eye.
Post coital fall-out like ash from Pompeii,
the silent ephemera of his infidelity.

West Lodge
Kirkton of Skene
April 2001

REBECCA JONES

11

Barbie Yaga

I put the kettle on, set out two cups and picked the teapot up. Then I sighed, put the teapot down, returned one cup to the cupboard and stuck a teabag in the other. Three months on and I still went through this pantomime about once a week. I had lived alone for years before meeting Fiona, but after five years with her I seemed to have lost the trick of it. I couldn't even play patience without expecting to hear her unsolicited advice. 'Seven on the eight and then the ace can go up.' It used to irritate the hell out of me. And as for nights, they were the worst. It should be easier to sleep soundly on your own, with no little noises and no competition for the duvet. It really should.

My self-pitying musings were interrupted by a delicate sneezing, the sort of sound you might hear if the world's unluckiest flower fairy had hay fever. I turned round and looked into the opposite corner of the kitchen, from where the sound had come. A tiny woman, about the size of a Barbie doll, was crouching in my mortar, trying to stifle her sneezes. I blinked and pinched myself, but she was still there. She stepped out of the mortar, got herself under control and stood up straight. Her figure was a bit full for a Barbie and her hair was dark, but she carried a sexual charge that would have reduced Ken to a steaming puddle of plastic.

Great! Now I'm hallucinating. My new anti-depressants must be strong stuff.

She gave me a long, measuring look and then spoke - in English, but with an accent, Eastern European perhaps.

'Don't you ever clean this thing?'

She was talking about the mortar, in which I had been pounding and mixing spices for the curry that had been dinner earlier that evening. It had also been dinner the night before - food for one was another thing I hadn't quite got the hang of. The smell of cumin and coriander mixed with her own feminine scent, but it was probably the pepper that had made her sneeze.

I've taken the trouble to imagine her, so I might as well speak to her.

'You sound just like my wife.'

In fact, she looked a bit like Fiona, too. Well, a Fiona airbrushed to perfection. A Fiona not pregnant with someone else's child.

'You have a wife? She puts up with this?'

She held her hand palm up and swung her arm in a horizontal arc to indicate that she referred to the state of the kitchen. Dirty dishes stacked in the sink. Unwashed pots on a stained and greasy hob. Empty bottles and used teabags strewn about haphazardly. There was so much dropped food on the lino that you could have tipped it into a pot and made a hearty broth.

'No, she left me. She puts up with whatever happens at the house of one Fraser McKay.'

'This Fraser McKay is he a prince - or a warrior - or some kind of sorcerer?'

'To hear Fiona talk, he's all three. But no, he's the second McKay of McKay, McKay and Finnie, solicitors. And he's the bastard who shagged my wife, got her pregnant and took her away!'

'If he's not a prince, a warrior or a sorcerer, why can't you just kill him?'

13

'Kill him! Yeah, great idea!'

Come on - get a grip. Never argue with a hallucination on its own terms.

'Just who…uh… what are you anyway?'

She strode to the edge of the worktop and gave me a hard stare. 'Don't they teach humans anything these days? Who do you think travels by mortar?'

I had to hand it to my subconscious; it knew its Russian folk tales. My conscious knowledge was learned reading stories to my niece. Her Barbie was often cast as Vasilisa the Beautiful or the Raisa who loved Finista the Falcon, but never as…

'Baba Yaga? Flying through the night in a mortar, causing women to miscarry and milk to sour?'

'Your great-grandson may call me Baba, although I'll need a bigger mortar by then. Otherwise you've got it about right.'

'Well, you're not up to date with social mores. Killing solicitors is considered bad form these days.'

'Indeed? In Scotland, perhaps. If respect for wise women has not also gone out of fashion, then you can wash this mortar and pestle for me.'

I would have asked her what the magic word was, but I was afraid that she might tell me the one that turns disrespectful humans into lizards. I made enough space in the sink to run the things under the hot tap and then wiped them dry with a paper towel. The little witch got back into the mortar and accepted the pestle from my outstretched hand.

'Now if you'll just open the window, I can fly out without breaking it.'

'Here you go', I said, complying. I could always buy another mortar and pestle tomorrow.

'One good turn deserves another. Before I leave, is there anything I can do for you?'

If you were about fifteen times bigger.

Then frustrated lust gave way to futile bitterness.

'You could fly over 27 Springwell Gardens, Morningside.'

Sex and revenge, two fantasies rolled into one.

'As long as that wouldn't be bad form.'

She gave a mischievous wink, tapped the pestle three times against the side of the mortar and flew out of the open window and into the night.

Slowly my mind seemed to clear, as if I had just awoken from a dream-ridden sleep. The Barbie Yaga was gone, as were my mortar and pestle. So I'd hallucinated and thrown some kitchen implements out of the window - big deal. Tomorrow I'd see the doctor about changing my prescription: for now, I had unfinished business with a cup of tea. I re-boiled the kettle, poured in the water and massaged the bag with a spoon. When I was happy with the strength, I fished out the bag and added it to my collection. Three spoonfuls of sugar, stirred nine times clockwise and the same back. Then I went to the fridge, but the milk had gone off.

ROBERT MCKAY LOTHIAN

In the morning I'll be glad

for the rain
that's stopped tumbling

for the light that blasts
my window

for the dreams that spark
my vision

and for the smell of your
wet skin

that I didn't touch

when your champagne eyes
fizzed into mine

CATRIONA YULE

Seminary

My mother baked them cakes:
wrestling with cold God.
Yet they sped right back,
to Him and stone walls
from our cosy living room.

Every week we watched
their hair flash the corner.
God: a knackered mortal,
weighed down in the ring,
sweating from her punches.

He was no match for her.
One by one, they settled
in different clothes,
out of priesthood,
nurturing their young,

no doubt telling offspring
about the woman
who sold them a line
with her Tango Sponge.

CATRIONA YULE

The Loch Ness Mystery

When she left a dead fish at my door
I thought, "There's plenty more
Where that one came from".

Once upon a time at Fort Augustus
I saw something bigger and more alive
But it moved off in the black water
Never to return.

It had all made perfect sense
When she peeled a layer of skin
From her sunburnt shoulder
And held it up to the light.

Biology held the answers to that
But love had other plans for us.

STEVE PORTER

Race to the End of the Road

I linger on this stretch of road.
We had to make an emergency stop
because our dog Mojo (a black magic charm)
shat on my sister's coat.

There was nothing lucky about that
and when the coat went out
only the dog's charm kept him in.

By the Strathisla, cattle won rosettes.
We came to see Miss Aberdeen Angus 1982.

At the vintage car auction, I caught fever
and my chauffeur drove through the night
in a Rolls Royce Silver Ghost.

In a Rolls Royce Silver Ghost,
my drunk old girl
in heels and a white dress,
tuned in to 'Three Little Birds'.

On the long straight at Lhanbryde
Dad wondered if he could do a ton
with his seventy-year-old father in the passenger's seat -
three generations sped towards the Oakwood,
red leaves on the road home.

STEVE PORTER

Nothing to Declare

Selina disboards the plane and follows the tunnelled walkway into the airport. **Welcome to Canada** adorns the curving wall in huge red letters next to a maple leaf.

The steady stream of fellow travellers slows to a halt, at the queue for **Passport Control**. Selina senses her heart rate increase slightly. She shows no outward signs of anxiety, though she knows the effect of the beta-blockers will have worn off by now.

She begins taking slow, deep breaths, just as Richard had advised. Her enhanced breasts make her feel top-heavy, as they stretch the fabric of her blouse with each expansion of her chest.

She'd been apprehensive at first. It was a dangerous operation, and Richard knew it. But he'd worn down her resistance with his countless telephone calls, pleading with her to do it *just for him.* And it was the thought of seeing him again, so soon, that had made her determined to go through with it.

He'd been anxious that she make it over in time for Burns night. He was to host the supper for the local appreciation society, and he wanted Selina to join him.

The queue moves forward a few steps at a time, and as she waits, Selina thinks back to the start of her journey - Aberdeen, the previous day. It seems like a lifetime ago that she'd approached that check-in desk.

'Did you pack these bags yourself?' the girl had asked. Selina had looked at the painted doll behind the counter, catching a waft of Chanel.

'Yes.'

'And has your luggage been left unattended at any time?'

'No.'

The girl fastened an adhesive label to the handle of each bag, before activating the conveyor. She took a boarding pass from the printer, and handed it to Selina along with her passport. 'Departure gate seventeen,' she smiled.

Selina took them, her hand steady as a rock. Inside, she was crumbling.

The x-ray machine was no problem, and she had nothing to fear from the walk-through metal-detector, but waiting her turn to be patted down by the zealous butch female at the departure gate had her rigid with terror. If she was to be exposed by those probing hands...

She fought an impulse to retreat, to run to a washroom. *There are eyes and ears everywhere in an airport*, Richard had warned her. She must retain her demeanour at all times.

To her relief, she was waved through with no more than a brief frisking. She vented a long sigh as she flopped down onto a seat in the departure lounge, and waited for the call to board.

****

Now she stands once more. A different country. A different queue. At the desk, a serious-looking official compares Selina's six-year-old passport photograph with her pallid face.

'Okay,' he smiles suddenly, hands the passport back to Selina, 'enjoy your stay.'

At **Customs and Excise**, Selina opts for **Nothing to Declare**. Her heart lurches at the sight of the two grim-faced men who scrutinise each traveller in turn. Selina gets ready with her best smile, but the men are not interested in her. Liberated, she heads for **Baggage Collection.**

****

Richard waits for her outside in a hired car. She gets in and he leans across until their lips touch. He cups a hand over her breast, squeezing gently.

'Hmm, nice,' he says. Can't wait to see them.'

Inside his apartment, Selina removes her coat then joins Richard in the kitchen. He hands her a glass of champagne, then, impatiently, takes it back and sets it on the table.

'Come on then,' he says, 'get them out.'

'Okay,' Selina agrees, eager to unburden herself. She pulls her top off and drops it on a chair. Richard holds both cups of her sports-bra in his hands, as Selina unhitches the catch at the back.

He takes it off, carefully, and places it on the counter. Selina unpeels the sticky tapes from inside each cup, to release the contents.

'Oh, yes, Babe,' Richard declares, 'You're a star!' He holds up a plump, five-hundred gram package in each hand. 'Wow,' he declares, 'these little beauties'll go down a treat at the Burns Supper,' and reading from the label of one, he quotes;

'One-Hundred-Percent Genuine Scottish Haggis…'

CAL WALLACE

Suburban Sentries

Noon drifts into
Friday's suburbia,
a terrace of houses
stands silent and calm.
Adults, at work,
dream of Utopia
where four day weekends
are always the norm.
Children, at school,
can't wait for release.
Others, in residence,
enjoy short lived peace.

Grey, foursquare, sentries
watch over this scene.
They wait, full to bursting,
with stuff that seemed
to be briefly of value.
Misjudgements and failures
consigned to their care,
a week's mess absorbed
leaving consciences bare.

For once, all is well
in Friday's suburbia.

Fleetingly.

RICHARD L. ANDERSON

In Praise of 2005

Fareweel!!
Ye wabbit dried oot scunner.
God save
ah live tae see a hunner
the likes o' you.

They'd scart ma erse
thon journal pages,
whaurin ah've scribed
ma rants an rages
against this world.

Stapped fou'
wi' death an disappointment,
conferred by them
scant praise anointed
ow'r us tae grieve.

Ma een wir blint
by yon bricht Simmer
that vouchsafed warmth
would last forever,
and masked cauld truth.

An noo yir loused
yiv left the riddle.
Whit divilish curse
in twel' months' travail
turns hope's milk soor ?

RICHARD L. ANDERSON

Caught Between a Rock and a Hard Place

The night crept in chilly and sinister, as gale-force winds pulled at the leaves. The branches thrashed like lunatics' arms desperate to ward off winter's inevitable straightjacket.

In this beastly darkness a young girl sunk deep into her jacket, grimacing. The wind rattled her bones but she took comfort in it. Deidra knew nothing or no one was going to stop her tonight. They would all be sheltering within the sallow walls of Ithaca Care Home. The others would have drawn their blankets up over their noses like highway robbers, defrosting their faces with their own breath. On such a spiteful night Matron would be listening to Radio 4, hot water bottle at her back, hot cocoa in her hand, bundle of keys on the bedside table. The porter would be warming his frosty heart with the *Jack Daniels* Deidra had slipped in the top drawer of his desk earlier that evening. Matron wouldn't miss the bottle. She only got the booze out when the inspectors came. Deidra's hollow footsteps echoed on the slimy cobblestones. She turned the corner.

Something scuttled behind a wheelie bin wedged in the corner of the back alley. The bin was bulging with garbage, mostly food thrown out by the Greek restaurant on the High Street. The flaps, claimed in coarse graffiti by *Stevie*, clanged on the sides. Deidra looked around.

She was sure this was the place.

Seafarer's Wynd. This was the place the woman had mentioned. The one in Slain's Rock, hiding her face in the shadows of the leather pew. The glimpse of that ashen face - blood-red lips and empty eyes - had haunted her dreams ever since the meeting three days ago.

The first she knew about Delphia, that had been the crone's name, was a small ad in the Evening Express. *Delphia, sorcerer of the truth.* That was all. That, and a phone number. She had barely registered it at first. But as she lay in bed she kept seeing the words as they danced on her grey wall. It was tempting, finding the truth. She had just celebrated another birthday where nobody turned up. No mother, no father, no sisters or brothers. Why couldn't anyone tell her who her family was? Why *wouldn't* they? In the end she had braved the linoleum on her bare feet and stolen into the kitchen. The paper had already been chucked out with the potato peelings but she did not mind a bit of filth. She'd torn out the ad and phoned, using her last credit.

She was after the truth of her past. The truth that was, she was sure, locked away deep in Matron's stone heart. Not one bit of information had ever leaked when she eavesdropped outside the staffroom. No notes in the office ever referred to her family. And she had scavenged those files often enough. In fact, her file was remarkably empty, just a baby photo. Not even a birth certificate. There were no clues in shoeboxes or lockets tucked away in safes. All she had was her name. Deidra - the wanderer.

'Sssssearching for sssomething?'

The hissing voice behind her made Deidra's neck hair stand to attention. She turned round. Staring at her were two bulging sapphire eyes framed by hair as dry as straw and streaked blue. Deidra drew in a breath.

'Sssshhh, is it Scylla the little girl seeks? Scylla she needs?' the creature drooled, opening the slit of its mouth to show three rows of pointy teeth. Deidra felt a coldness seeping up from the ground. The creature stretched out a bony hand, and touched Deidra's cheek with webbed fingers. Deidra stepped back. What was this creature?

'Or is it Charybdis? Maybe it is Charybdis you look for. Hahaha!' Deidra's heart froze when she heard the icy voice. She turned round. She gasped and shut her eyes. Above her loomed a giant of a woman, built like a sumo wrestler, with hair flowing round her head like water. Her mouth was a gaping black hole. Hollow laughter rolled through the alley. Charybdis held her sides as her belly shuddered. Scylla scuttled close.

'Girl sssay it, girl sssay it. Is it Ssscylla, is it Charybdissss?'

The two creatures closed in on Deidra. What should she say? Would she be in trouble if she chose one over the other? She was caught between a rock and a hard place. All Delphia had said was to get here tonight, at 11.30. She didn't expect to meet two people, if they were people. All she had come for was the answer to the secret.

She managed to squeak, 'Delphia sent me,' annoyed at the babyish tremor in her voice. 'I came to find out the truth about my parents. Can you help? Either of you?'

'Tss, tsss,' Scylla lisped,' yes. Scylla help little girl, but it costsss.'

Charybdis squeezed her arms around Deidra. 'Are you prepared to pay?'

Deidra gasped for breath. She tried to wriggle loose, shuffling her feet. She felt her pocket for the money she had stolen from the petty cash box. 'I'll pay.' Charybdis let go of her. Deidra fell on her knees, unprepared for the sudden release.

'Girl sssilly, ssssilly girl. Ssstinky money no pay for secret. Only silence…' Scylla floated around Deidra staring at her with a hypnotic gaze. She plucked at Deidra, licking her fingers after. 'Mmmmm, nice girl. Scylla hungry. Charybdis explain.'

Charybdis blocked the way out of the alley. 'Here's our offer. We will show you the answer to your question but you must not tell a soul.'

'Never tell. Sssecret. Sssecret sssacred,' echoed Scylla.

Charybdis continued. 'If you do, we will find you. I will have your sight and you will live a life of darkness. Scylla will have your tongue, and you will live a life of silence. Do you understand?'

'Silly girl see it? See secret now?' Scylla moved around Deidra like a belly dancer.

Charybdis folded her arms and roared. 'Do you want to know the answer bad enough? Is it worth the risk? Remember, you must not tell a soul. Hahaha…'

Deidra hesitated. So even if her parents were alive she couldn't ever tell them. Maybe it was better never to find out. But to know! Eleven lonely years. Eleven years of wondering and fantasizing. She had to know. Better to know and never tell. 'You're on.'

Scylla grabbed her arm. Deidra winced at the sharp nails digging through her Puffa as she was dragged deeper into the dingy alleyway. A small fire was flickering in a waste bin. It threw up huge shadows on the wet wall bending over them. In the distance Deidra could hear steps, a quickening of pace, the rattle of keys. Someone was coming. She faced Scylla and Charybdis.

'Tell me who I am. Who are my mother and father.'

'Remember, you can never tell.'

'I know. Never tell.'

Scylla's glass eyes glazed over as she murmured in a strange tongue. The chanting grew louder. Charybdis rocked back and forth, droning a low bass. Scylla dropped to her knees, perspiration trickled down her temples. Her voice rose in waves. The steps came closer.

'Deidra!'

Deidra glanced backwards. That voice - Matron! How did she find her? Oh no, not now. She was so close. Deidra urged Scylla and Charybdis on. 'Hurry, hurry, I haven't got much time.' Charybdis looked like she might throw up. Her body was jerking involuntarily. And then, suddenly, Scylla shrieked.

In the flames appeared a young woman. Deidra saw her clutching a pink bundle. The woman was crying and running. Behind the woman Deidra saw an angry man waving his fist. He was shouting something. His face looked black as thunder. He released a barking Doberman but the young woman had disappeared.

Deidra heard the steps falter, shuffle and then pick up again. Matron was running. The keys clanged loudly.

The scene changed. The young woman stood on the doorstep of a tall building. She held out a baby to an old woman in a black dress. The old woman smiled warmly but shook her head. Instead she beckoned in the young woman and the baby. She scanned the street carefully and then pulled the heavy door closed. On a sign next to it Deidra read *Ithaca*.

'Deidra! Be careful. Hold on!' The steps could be no further than around the corner.

Again the scene changed. She saw herself sitting in a window sill. And the woman, older now, observing her. She was wearing a grey trouser suit, blowing a steaming cup. Attached to her trousers was a bundle of keys.

Deidra let out a sob. She gazed ahead. Scylla and Charybdis had gone. The flames were shimmering. But the alley was empty.

'Deidra!' Matron turned her round roughly by the shoulder. 'What in Heaven's name do you think you're doing! It's the middle of the night. There's a storm brewing. You had me worried sick!' Deidra could hear Matron was nearly crying.

'Mum,' Deidra mumbled without thinking, still seeing the images from the flames. All those years, so close, and she had never known. Why? Then all went black. She tried to speak but could only gutter strange sounds.

Matron wrapped her up in a fleece. As she was led away, Deidra heard a sharp hissing. Matron glanced at the flash that lit up the sky and pulled Deidra closer. It was followed only seconds after by a low rumble that sounded like belly-rippling laughter.

PAULINA VANDERBILT

Wrong expert

Polite, I smile.
I ask a question.

Eyes slide sideways as light shines
on dank alleys they prefer to forget.

Acknowledge the past, they say,
and let it go. Ah yes…until…
Again, I ask my question.

The lines are busy; the question
lies there writhing in the blight
of knowledge. It will not die.

I smile. Polite,
I ask the question.

GRÁINNE SMITH

You said

I sang my heart out just for you.
You said, that song is most uncool.
I sang another straight and sore.
You said, I've heard those words somewhere before.
I sang the charts, long ballads, jazz.
I sang it high then tried it bass,
I sang it soft, I sang it loud,
I sang with beat, I sang off key
You said….you said….
What was that you said?

GRÁINNE SMITH

Wake

Blacks, grey, navy
mix with browns sitting on
plain polished wood.

Voices rise, thin,
muted, to the heights
of the arches.

The drum kit in the corner sulks,
hidden behind a grand piano, abandoned
in favour of the organ playing fugue.

For me,
       No black, no grey or navy,
       no muted browns
       or mourning notes
       fluting in the air.

For me,
       Play those drums,
       crash the cymbals,
       dance your fingers
       up the keys.

For me,
       Be brilliant
       in pink or red,
       purple, turquoise.

Pull out all the stops.
And sing, sing, sing.

GRÁINNE SMITH

"You Are Here"

At night, in a great ship's cabin, asleep and dreaming.
You wake up suddenly to the throbbing of distant machinery. The
vivid dream you inhabited seconds before is gone, its subject less
than a memory.
You reach for your constant companion, seeking reassurance
through familiar contact.
You climb over the edge of your bunk, and your bare feet on the
warm floor feel the ship's vibrations.
A pale blue mist of light bathes your confined space.
To provide sufficient natural ventilation under tropical latitudes, the
cabin door is left open but secured and yet clicking quietly with the
regular rocking of your transatlantic universe.
Squeezing through the gap with your companion in tow, you enter
the source of the blue light.
The corridor is like a flooded canyon; its perfect perspective
vanishes to its artificial horizon along never-ending nor widening
valleys where tributary junctions branch into cul-de-sacs.
Blueprint, no doubt by Daedalus, a great ship made in Krytos.
Without knowing, you pass the point of no return. You have lost
your way, no amount of backtracking through identical passages
can bring you back to the safety of your own cabin and without
Ariadne's thread the labyrinth has swallowed you both but you don't
know it yet.
Is this bliss by ignorance? And that Ariadne, her thread and the
labyrinth, who or what are they?

Do you wonder if the omnipresent pulsations emanate from a
Minotaur lurking beyond the next left turn or the first stairwell
going down?
But what is a Minotaur to you?
Unaware of questions for which you have no answer, you go on till
you reach an oasis of white light in the blue dusk. On the wall a
map, the plan of the labyrinth! And by luck at the bottom of the
plan, in an alphabet still foreign to your understanding, three
groups of signs with an arrow pointing to the heart of the maze.
Focus your sight and like the bumblebee that flies against all known
aerodynamical laws, read without knowing you can't.
"YOU...ARE...HERE...".
It's a miracle. You read it again.
The sentence maintains its message.
You examine each word in no particular order, having yet to be told
what are words and the mysterious way they work.
Nothing changes; the letters hold their individual position, self-
adding to their associative meaning or - as some used to pretend -
their cabalistic truth.
A minimalist three-word sentence, subject, verb and complement,
starting with a capital Y and reading like a universal truth.
Puzzled by the revelation of such potential message enclosed within
three words, you find it impossible to proceed with your
Peregrination.
Then the mystery reaches you.
The veil starts to part, is it ISIS? Epiphanies? Isis Unveiled?
The quest moves on returning with that first YOU word.
Who is, or who are included in that YOU?

YOU? Internally you answer ME? Secretly hoping your ME doesn't correspond to their YOU! Unless your friend is counted.
You are not old enough to be one of them.
You tighten your hold on your passive companion.
The second word claims that you ARE, a situation tied to the great alternatives of being.

You remember, without having been told, about a mythical Danish Prince, or more accurately about his literary creator.
It is a common fault to attribute the lines spoken by characters to their actors when the writer is the only culprit.
And still you ARE without the precision of whom or what, again you have no satisfying answer and if you thought you knew, millions of other beings will instantly disagree.
The last word proclaims a location, HERE.
A place of transit at best, eternally present in the past as in the future.
The centre, since on a sphere any point is located at the centre of its surface, the antipode and the middle of nowhere.

YOU...ARE...always HERE.

Like a surrealist slide show, metaphors flash rapidly past.
You catch one, a colourful kinescope format showing a far paradise
by a wounded artist, who knew VAN GOGH, a sharp frozen
shaving-mirror.
Automatically the depth of your unconscious reasoning makes your
palms sweat.
You drop the mysterious companion that only a minute ago you had
clutched tightly for comfort.
Then the last blow as you remember that you never learned to read.
You freeze mesmerised by the implication of your discovery.
You unload to subconscious all recent memory without retrieval
index entries.
Empty daydream blocks your mind till audio function detects a
voice calling your name.
Then a familiar face lowers itself to your level.
Two arms lift you as you heard the three magic words in a new
order:

"Here You Are!"
And then "You dropped Dumbo!"

MICHEL DUDROPT

from **Kaleidoscope : A sequence of nine poems**

vi

Between the coffins which bear his children's bodies
he stands, holding the weapon between his hands.
Disked, bladed, a man's palm's width (no more).
Like a food processor part, or something else
domestic, outsourced, mass-produced, cheap.
An A-10's avionics saw his children
hide behind an outhouse in his yard
but not that they were playing, nor that they
were children. Cluster launched, their deaths became
this image: monochrome, softly-lit, still:
within which he, purported calm surpassing
all understanding, holds the weapon which lopped
(as specified) the tops from both his children's skulls.

Downstairs, I hear our tumble dryer spin.

viii

His chest crackles for each indifferent doctor's
ear. How many x-rays, drugs before it's clear?
He bathes to the suck of lungs loosening, for
an hour, the residue of his escape:
until they pack back down as water cools.
Two months 'til his insurance stops. The talk
of war seems spectacularly pointless.
Everywhere he feels eyed, sideways.
                                    One AM.
To let his partner sleep, he walks the site,
sees his shallow rasp dissolve in air he
finds some resolution in. His iPod plays
Zep IV - all ambient, ironic depth.
When the levee breaks, got no place to stay.
Those drums. He smiles at the last twisted steels.

IAN MORRISON

Hunters and Collectors

Peacock proud and dressed to thrill,
Strutting night streets, bold as brass.
Trip through light on heels fantastic,
Tiredly queuing - all clubbed out.
Sun tattooed on small backs arching
Golden shaded models catwalk.
Careless howls in winter's traffic,
Claws concealed in sleeveless furs.
Displaying multi-styles and hues,
Crows and magpies, raccoon tails.
Pouting, posing, would be wannabes
Auditionees for news film footage.
Raking at prospective rivals,
Potential spouses stunned look on.
Catfights on the cobbles' icing,
Falling short of falling apart.

MARK PITHIE

The Race of Life

Holding hands with some reluctance
You and I aged four or five

Going shopping with our mothers
Hand in hand on Union Street

Infant faces forcing smiles
Dragged young feet at Kodak's clicking

Starting right with T-bar sandals
On our marks to start our lives

The human race was run before us
By grown-ups like our Mums and Dads

As Union Street stretched out before us
We were sure we'd go the distance

MARK PITHIE

Torture at Tyrebagger

She says it's like one of those stupid trust exercises on management training courses. Only the exercise is – do you trust yourself? And with that she confiscates my pocket torch. The entrance tunnel is only about five feet long but it bends halfway so that no light follows you in, and there's almost no light inside. Three feet in I decide the answer's no; and I can picture her lounging outside knowing that, secretly, I can't stand the dark, and knowing even better that I'm never going to admit that and turn back.

The tunnel ends and there's empty blackness all round me, which is even worse. The space smells powerfully organic. I edge forward thinking of all the woodland creatures - rabbits, foxes, badgers – that might be in here, alive or dead. Or the birds that could have flown in and not have been able to get back out. I remember the summer I was six, when we found a dead crow in the garden - intact, glossy, but strangely misshapen and squirming with maggots. We took turns at holding it, at arms length, by the tip of its dislocated wing until my mum came and ordered us all inside to wash our hands. Now with every step forward I'm expecting to feel the soft crunch of feathers and maggots underfoot.

When my foot touches the central wooden platform I sigh with relief and realise that I've been all but holding my breath in the interim. Contact with something at least partially manmade is hugely reassuring. Then I remind myself that the whole thing is manmade. That's the point. A funfair haunted house dressed up as art. I start to wonder if this is her idea of revenge for my refusal to attend the art gallery opening last week.

Standing near the centre, in the thin shaft of light that comes from the single, 10p piece sized hole in the roof, my eyes slowly adjust and I can almost make out the sloping stone walls of the chamber, only a few feet away. Just as I think I've steeled myself to step off the platform towards one, the faint light disappears entirely, returns briefly and is blocked out again. As the initial panic subsides I discern, in the camera obscura effect the light creates on the platform, the shape of a hand waving back and forth.

"Bitch," I mutter. The word does not echo as I expect, the stone chamber swallows it whole.

The worst is over then. When I hear rustling in the tunnel a few moments later I know it's only her coming to join me. We stand together on the platform, watching the play of shadows made by the trees and clouds above us in the outside world, and I see how this could be romantic. Almost. If it wasn't for the smell and the dripping damp and the shadowy, but no doubt ecologically active, corners. The return journey through the tunnel is barely better and I am profoundly grateful when I emerge into the midge ridden air, which only twenty minutes before I had cursed as a hellish environment to spend a Saturday in.

Of course there's still the rest of the trail to go. Trudging along miles of tracks that alternate through humid forest and the ugly stubble of cleared pine trees. Puzzling over whose idea it was to hide brass slugs and clusters of aluminium rods amid a perfectly inoffensive stretch of kitchen units and bedroom furniture in waiting.

After three hours we finally make it back to the car park, and in my haste to get away I almost reverse the Focus into a tree trunk. When we're finally on our way I tell her that next weekend we're bloody well going to Ikea, like everyone else.

ELAINE KAY

43

Eggshells

A blizzard was raging the day he came to visit
a special Northern show
He took a photo of a fourteenth century chapel
a stark tree and him in ski gloves and a thin jacket

In the house we sat before a coal fire
eating his dates and listening to his tape
of Arab music, and he asked
which way pointed East

At breakfast he tried to peel his soft-boiled egg
dropping bits of shell into the egg cup
like bits of Western culture
We watched and waited for the yolk to burst

At the bus station we stood with him in the wind
warming each other with our smiles
and as he said goodbye he squeezed our hands

OLIVIA MACMAHON

Metamorphosis

Suddenly Apollo's there, quivering.

A God's gift. I spring to my feet,

flee into the woods. *Oh save me, my father,*

my River God father. Don't leave me to this death.

Apollo's breath is hot behind me.

But I might have guessed my Dad would be hopeless

in dealing with such a situation.

He turns me into a tree. My feet take root,

my skin I was so proud of thickens,

my arms are fixed in helpless splendour,

and Apollo's making for himself a wreath

out of the leaves that were my fingers.

Oh, why could you not have armed me, father?

Turned me - fleetingly - into a cobra?

OLIVIA MACMAHON

The Banishing

'Go,' he said.

Was it that he'd grown tired of them,
their presence in his garden,
lounging under the apple blossom,
by the shimmering stream
with the wind's breath upon them?

Or maybe it was their silent reproaches:
Why do you leave us so much alone,
long days passed, waiting your return?
Maybe he'd sensed
their loneliness.

It took them a while to isolate
the probable moment of their undoing,
the day he'd come down from the mountain,
smiling but stern,
and they'd ventured to speak.

OLIVIA MACMAHON

The National Hyperbaric Centre

Mention the word 'hyperbaric' and what springs to mind is the treatment of divers suffering from the 'bends', an unpleasant condition caused by the diver surfacing too quickly and requiring immediate treatment in a decompression chamber.

The National Hyperbaric Centre in Aberdeen, situated in the grounds of Aberdeen Royal Infirmary was opened in 1987 by Lord Cecil Parkinson several years after it was seriously mooted and after some controversy as to planning permission. Grampian Regional Council for instance was concerned that the proposed Centre would detract from the amenity of their Woodhill House Headquarters. The Centre maintains an emergency service for divers who may be in need of extensive medical or surgical assistance, which was the original concept. The NHC is a deep-water simulation facility comprising a steel vessel where deep water conditions can be created and is useful for research and development of work associated with diving including the testing of diving suits.

In 1990 Tom Shields, Senior Consultant at the Centre maintained that the Centre was not being fully utilised and hyperbaric medicine (the exposure of patients to highly pressurised oxygen) could save the lives of people normally beyond standard treatment, e.g. those with skin ulcers, problem wounds, skin grafts, etc. At the time, the Health Board was reluctant to fund the treatment of patients other than divers, and even commissioned a report which convinced doctors that such treatment was useless, but fortunately, over the years, this attitude has changed and most consultants and doctors will refer to the Centre such patients for whom treatment could be beneficial.

The Aberdeen Unit is classed by the British Hyperbaric Association as Category 1 and is the only one in Scotland capable of providing intensive care support in a hyperbaric environment. The Unit has access to a helipad for the reception of casualties by helicopter from distant locations and is especially useful for divers working from oil rigs when they cannot be treated by the oil companies' own staff. There is a dedicated staff and all activity is carefully monitored by nurses from the Aberdeen Royal Infirmary's Intensive Therapy Unit, who have been specially trained in hyperbaric nursing in addition to their critical care training.

The chamber is quite large, approximately 6.3 metres long and 2 metres high and wide, plenty of room for moving about. Inside the chamber there are 3 beds and one folding chair and the patient may sit or lie down, whichever is more comfortable. The oxygen is given to the patient through a hood resembling a clear plastic spaceman's helmet that has a safe neck seal, all the time being carefully monitored. Comfortable cotton trousers and top and special anti-static shoes are provided in place of the patients' own clothes when they enter the Unit. Treatment is painless apart from an uncomfortable 'popping' in the ears, similar to that experienced in aircraft, for the short time that the oxygen is pumped into the helmet. The sessions last usually for two and a half hours and the consultant will have discussed with you the number of sessions you will require. A session may require to be cancelled should a diver require emergency treatment but the Unit staff will give you warning of this.

It has now been proved that hyperbaric treatment is beneficial to some patients, and it is hoped that the Unit will continue to treat such patients who may previously have had little hope of recovery.

ANN NICOL

A lifetime

The wasps' nest,
ensconced inside a splintered window beam
– sunbathed and restful like a summer house.

The colony must have been small.
Each time one, at most two individuals,
emerge drumming on the wooden beam

to tune their wing cases in gleams to the breeze
  Minute...
tending the sleep, the welfare of the young ones
  ... and meticulous.

The summer's still in its prime.
Repairs have lent the byke
an unblemished façade.

JOSÉ SOLERA

Neighbour-san

Flanked by dim desk light,
thrown-open books, a rugged globe;
reading top to bottom, right
to left, scholarly at peace.

I, tapping out into daylight,
meet his round smile again,
his appointed good-morrow
from behind the bamboo canes.

Aberdeen, solitude

Lonely lighthouse blinks afar.
In between a mirage stands
As the tide breathes out the haar
Pungent with sea-weeds and salty sand.

JOSÉ SOLERA

Glenelg

The swinging weight
Of foot in boot
Pulls my body forward.

Senses, like boxed heirlooms, unwrap,
Tissues whipped away by clammy buffets of wind.

Irritable scrub twitches,
Grey whiskers jerking on dark young skeletons.

A stump, upholstered in chartreuse velour
Shouts an optical yahoo.

Over the lochan a heron carves an arc,
Then sways on a lace bush.

A slither of root,
Black and slick as an eel,
Humps the ground.

And a dead sheep snorkels in a bog,
Caught between rocks, in a soft place.

2004

MARIANNE NICOLL

Inverkeilor

Willowherb straggles along the high bank,
Blousey finery and plumes gone.
Scissoring ribs now carry shredded pennants.

A barley plant, caught in the buff
And out of time,
Shivers at the edge of a newly ploughed field.

Flat farmland slopes to the coast
Where huddles of naked willow stems shield a stream,
Old growth grey,
This year's amber in the low sunshine.

On the lee face of a wall, figures of lichen freeze
In a monochromatic dance.

Stones on the shore, of dun and dove and pewter,
Rub their faces in the daily grind,
Granite against sandstone,
Slate against basalt.

Through them all an icy wind shouts and rushes.

A silhouette stands on a wart of rock beyond the shoreline,
Shoulders hunched against the wind,
His back to the bare facts.

2004

MARIANNE NICOLL

Mind the Gap

A beer, a grilled sausage with a dab of mustard, as the crowds flow and pass. The air is warm and filled with the smells of hot metal, oil, the reheated food of half a dozen countries.

The lights in rows all point to the darkness beyond the end of the station, out of which a train appears. It slows and stops, disgorging a new stream of passengers who stride forth, eyes fixed on their goal, except for those few who wander uncertainly, looking for some clue, some direction.

Where are we? We are in München, in Paris, in Roma. We are in Tokyo, New York, Rio. We have been here before. Or we have always been here. Always will be.

Each of us once stepped from that train, without knowing where to go next, with no signpost to guide us, no-one to meet us and take us onward. We exist where others pass, remain where others go on, for wherever we go is here.

For my part, I was on my way, and knew where I was to go. Does it matter where? There was a connection, or was not, which is more to the point. There, and then, where and when one leg of a journey ended and the next began, between platforms, in the gap between arrival and departure, I stuck.

Is it chance alone that takes us and removes us from the moving world? Or is there a gene, a trait, a family quirk?

My uncle was a wanderer. He went with friends one summer to pick grapes in France. Then somebody suggested a trip to Istanbul. Before he knew it he was in India, his passport blazoned with visas, his mind expanded. Indonesia was followed by Australia, America, South and North, until, grown in body and mind, he returned.

"I've got the travelling out of my system now." He picked up his education, career, seemed settled. But there was an itch. Watching an aeroplane cross the sky above his head one day, he cracked. In twenty-four hours he was on a train to Portugal. Why Portugal? Why not?

But my uncle is not me. He found his way back, and though now he disappears, irregularly, as the fit takes him, he comes back, in days, or weeks, but he finds his way there and he finds his way back.

I thought I knew what drove him, once.

To see a girl I liked, I had to change trains at Oberhausen. As I waited for the red snail of a local train, across the lines I could always see a huge green and gold steed, panting and shivering with anticipation. It had come from carnivals in Venice, and would soon, soon, be released to run through the night, through the plains, across the streams, amid the hills, all the way to Saint Petersburg.

I had money. I had my passport, as always. I had not the nerve.

Is that what happened, later, when I became lost? Did I find the nerve, just at the moment when going there shifted to coming here? I could show you the spot, but it would not be the same spot, for the time is different, the moment is gone; the spot where I found there was to be no connection, and finding that, fell between the old, dependable, and the new, the unknown, to land here in the gap between the end of today and the beginning of tomorrow.

I knew what is was, once, to travel towards, with an aim, an objective, a place to explore, or re-explore. Now the direction has escaped me, the grail has faded, from sight, from memory, and has become less than myth, a whisper from a forgotten dream.

Here is home now. Home, they say, is where they will always take you back. That is true of here. Here is where I am at home. Where I feel least uncomfortable.

The passengers have dispersed, the ones with destinations in their sights long gone, the others, who had to seek their objectives, they too have drifted away, finding the directions, the clues they sought.

Every now and then, with one in ten thousand, no, a hundred thousand, I see the look that says, "Yes I am here, and here again, different yet the same. I am always here, wherever here is."

Then I see that you are like me. Fallen from the world which moves, left between trains.

AIDAN MULKERRIN

red evening

eyes sufficiently closed
all the world was bathing
in the red beneath the lids
of some imagined immortal

swimming through vermilion
air thick as water
Pinot Noir the prism
firewood the smell

gentle was our moving
though urgent in its nature
held back and exquisite
greater and more profound

sounds of broken rollers
dashing upon the shore
scent the waves and waves
of dulcet brunette rings

all was naked twilight
all was now but going down
and going down
was but half the journey

our sounds were elemental
language immaterial
skin suffused with meaning
hello hello hello hello

in the locus now
we are focussed now
both present –
tick the register

yes miss - paying attention …
yes sir - paying attention…

the night is coming
and we are here…

KNOTBROOK TAYLOR

Bar Shark

Swimming, swimming, swimming. If I stop swimming I firmly believe I will drown. I'll sink down into that deep dark that haunts me. For now, this is not a problem. Swimming is easy. Swimming is what I do and I do it so well. In and out of the clubs and bars, with the tide or against the current, it's all the same to me. Over the tables, between the stools, among all the pretty fish. At a distance I circle and watch and wait. There is an art to waiting. I haunt the shoal until I smell that smell. I can smell a pretty fish before I see her. She may be clean, she may be soaked in perfume, but she can't hide that scent. That so subtle signal, that tells me when she is ready to be taken. Loneliness cast like a shadow across her pointless, gulping face. When she is filled to the gills with need and her drink of choice, when she moves to the edge of the shoal, that's when I strike. A flick of the tail, I'm there. All teeth and trapping, I lose the deadness in my eye. It's that moment, in a conversation, when words do my dirty work. When smiles belie what I really want. Because what I really want is meat. I will do practically anything to get my prey. If you want a nice guy, I will renounce my tribe. If you want mean, I can do that. You want to laugh, I'll swim on my back and roll my eyes into the top of my head. The result will be the same. You see, I know who you are. I've been doing this for a very long time. I'm from those unforgiving seas and they have taught me how to hunt, how to feel the vibrations, and to follow that trail of bubbles to its source. I need you. I hate you. I can tell the hunger in a room, see the hunger in your eyes, the hunger in your soul. It's that same hunger which drives me on, and on, through these dim lit places, swimming these fascinating waters, searching for the next pretty fish, the next silhouette, the next moment to defy the dark. Swimming, swimming, swimming.

KNOTBROOK TAYLOR

November Night

The rainiest, most misrubble November ever, don-cha think? I mean, crappy weathur belongs in Janyery. They ur the rules, man – you know, when you're skint aftur Chrismiss and aw that – you just stay in a lot wi cut price beers that the offy didny manage to shift at New Year – an' the wind's at it ootside and you're inside wi your mates roun to watch DVDs and late night TV and maybe a bitty porn, even. But THIS? This is takin the piss, man! It's freezin, it's not on, man.

He's drunk again. That makes him more vocal than normal and a weather expert no less! Right enough, for once he does have a point. I keep thinking I'm in Glasgow – that someone shifted me during the night, and I wake up to sounds I'm not used to hearing here, sounds that take me back to a time I can hardly remember and somehow I'll never forget either. It's sunk in my consciousness, just like it took me six months to stop carrying an umbrella everywhere I went because I couldn't quite believe that I just wasn't likely to need it.

It's gonny snow, man. It's pure cold enough. I can sense it, I can feel it in the air. 'Member that night when we wur in Glencoe and I said it was gonny snow and it did – well, I git that same feeling agane. Ma fingers ur blocks uv ice. It's a frostbite situashin, I tell you.

Clairvoyant, now. What next? I just want to get home, and he's taking forever, and let's face it, I'm colder than he is, and I've got high heeled shoes on – he doesn't know he's born with Docs and chinos and a big coat. Wear a little dress, honey, he said. It's an occasion. Well, I suppose it was, my sister's wedding no less, but it's over now and I'm longing for bed, but I'll have to get him up the stairs first and then as soon as I'm undressed he'll be wanting sex and I'll have to talk him out of it. And he'll be all resentful – but if I give in and say okay, he'll end up mad because he's too drunk to do it. Either way he'll be annoyed at me. Maybe I should just leave him downstairs in his clothes. He'll be annoyed in the morning, but hey, he's an adult and since when was it my job to mother him?

If this rain wid just let up for a minnit, like, just wan MINNIT! Or the wind, man – why's it always misrubble when you canny git a taxi – an if the sun's cracking the flags there's a great long cue uv the damn hings. Always the same, eh, man. The wan hing you need is naewhere to be foun.

Great truths from the lips of the unaware. What we need we can't find or can't have. Maybe it's just because you want it so much that you notice it's not there, or maybe it's a perverse law of the modern world that people just aren't allowed to get their heart's desire. Maybe it's because we never say out loud what we want, we never dare tell anyone – we'd look too much like fools when it didn't materialise, it's safer just to moan on and on about what you have that you don't want – dead end jobs and scrubby flats and careless selfish boyfriends.

Ur we nearly there yit? I hope so, cos I'm COLD, man.

He's actually whining! He sounds like a kid in the back of a family's estate car when they're 15 miles into a 400-mile trip. Childish concept of a journey, innocent to the passing of time and all the tedium it entails. Too full of enthusiasm for the promised land, the destination and all the fun that's ahead. But that just doesn't apply here – we're at the bridge – less than ten minutes now, and when I get in I'm going to make a hot drink for myself – upstairs on that gadget tea-maker thing we never use. I've put up with quite enough tonight, so he can please himself. If he gets into bed dressed or something equally stupid, I'll sleep in the spare room. He can apologise in the morning.

Here we go, here we ur, man, at last.

He stands there, expectantly, like a little kid and I feel my irritation rise in seconds from grudging tolerance to near-rage. I have to rake around in his pockets for the keys and this is not good. He's shown me up in front of my mates, he's been rude to my parents – I'm biting my tongue not to say it all, because drunk ears are deaf, irrational. He stands there rocking on his heels while I struggle at the lock, strands of hair glued wetly cross my cheeks and neck. I'm so cold I hardly know I'm alive. Only anger keeps me going at moments like this: it boils up, an ugly thing. My patience is stretched so thin. All I have to look forward to is tomorrow's hangover and probable penitence, and I'm sick of this role, this rain, this cold, this maturity, this facing the fact of the less-than-wonderful nature of life.

And my single friends tonight envied me and I laughed and told them they were welcome to him. What did they see and hear? His rough good looks and his charming way of dealing out compliments about their dresses and hairdos. Me tactfully playing down the fact that I'd "done it" – got a guy – and they hadn't. But who could have guessed I was seriously willing to do a swap with any of them, flirt a little, have some fun, actually enjoy a conversation, get a little bit of male attention, feel a bit sexy after three years of being taken for granted, be kissed by a guy who saw it as getting lucky and not just his basic right and not knowing in advance how he would touch, if he'd be worth it or not.

I wrap the spare duvet around me and wonder if I could hack it again on the single circuit? Easy to recall the good bits when you're not dealing with the rejection and the fear and the surges of insane hope, paying for strappy sandals you know will murder your feet because you need to compete with the younger ones who can hack the pace, keep going all night, even if it is just because they're taking speed.

Which is the lesser of two evils? The devil you know, they say – well, I've met both devils and they're both pretty evil, and where are the guardian angels, that's what I want to know? Where on this miserable November night, as my senseless boyfriend crashes about in the kitchen downstairs, not even aware yet than I won't be sharing his beery morning breath, not this time, where are the guardian angels who'll help me get away from these twin devils that have chased me right out of my twenties and aren't giving me any peace in my thirties either. When do I get to be one of the happy people who know about love, not just about life, gritty old life, but love too – love, that old chestnut, that slippery, slidey illusion that seems to exist, but maybe it's just a cruel mirage, only ever out of reach.

Time to sleep now, I'm warm and cosy and it's all gone quiet down there, and I'm not bothered enough to go down and investigate, check he's not burning the house down with a cooker ring left on. Face tomorrow tomorrow, as they say, with all the ups and downs of life in the zeroes, the brave bright new century of nothingness and endless questions – and complaints about the miserable weather.

HELEN ELIZABETH RAMSEY

Irritant on a summer's day

Sitting in the sun, fully relaxed,
Almost, even, Afro-jointed.
Lazy sounds.   And where's the harm?

An ambling fly crosses my hand,
About its business, over my arm,
Then my face.   And who's to know?

Sudden, uptight consternation.
"My God! A fly on you!"
"Filthy beast!"   But it's mine to care.

What's the problem? Why the beefing?
Vicars, vegans, everybody,
"A fly! A fly!"   And such aggression.

Least of my worries, this I promise,
Flies, the very least,
On a day like this.

ROBERT RAMSAY

Mint Julep

Her veranda filled with husbands
Thickset German-Americans
Lolling, with cropped hair, wives at home -
Baking.

A hot evening on the Mason-Dixon, she
Cool in something floaty, slim
Her red hair fading
Buttermilk skin glowing in the kind light,
And blond wives home baking.

ROBERT RAMSAY

Momadu and the Sardine Fishers – *An extract*

I am Momadu. I am ten. I live in Goderich village. Me fadda tell me dis de biggest fishin' village in all de contry. Fish'men dey are comin' here from far an' wide. We get Temne, Susu, Mende, Kroo an' Bullom men, bot de most plenty are de Fante people. Dey are comin' from Ghana in de dry season, when de sardine com close to de beach. Never you see soch black black men. Som de elders dey say dis people bring bad magic, dey steal we fish, dey steal we titties. Bot me fadda, him tell me dem jost jealous because dem better fish'men. Me fadda say: "We Temne people, never we fish dis sardine before de Fante com, always we are fishin' bonga." Dat what we Temne people lek. Meself I de lek couta, de flesh him sweet pass all. Me modda she get good coppa for dis fish. Even de whitemen com here to buy um.

I want to be a fish'man. Me modda say I must go to school, bot I no de lek! Mr Ibrahim, he beat me too moch. Him say: "Where you' mind boy? You never pay attention, you always dreamin'! If you no listen, you no learn. If you no learn, you no get work." What him sabbe? Him no sabbe not'ing. I am *not* stupid, I *will* go to sea. Me fadda say always there is work for good seaman. When she hear dis, me modda, she de vex too moch.

"Why you go encourage de boy lek dat? Him jost end op anodder no-good black-arse fish'man lek him fadda."

"Who you callin' a no-good black-arse fishman? You get a wicked tongue, Susu woman!"

De both of them dey are shoutin'; dey have big palaver, den me fadda him grab me modda, give um big kiss. Him winkin' at me. Modda start to laugh, den we all laughin'. De storm don pass. Me fadda t'row me coins.

"Momadu, go buy two beer, de cold one from Ma Conteh. No com back too quick."

Door close behind me. In de hut I hear um say: "Now what dat you say about me black arse, Susu woman?"

Dem grown-up people, dem always havin' fon.

***

Me fadda get t'ree wife.

"Plenty problem!" him say, bot still him laughin'. Me modda, she de yongest one. I tink say him de lek her de best. Him say: "Dem Susu women, dey de best lookin' ones in all de world. Allah, him bake dem jost de right colour brown, lek we Temne people. Dem black, black Fante women, Allah don bake dem too moch. As for de white one, dem no baked at all." Me fadda say we must pity dem.

Ev'ry day me fadda bring home fish, bot him no stay ev'ry night. Some time him go to de hut of de second wife, Fatima. Dat one she get a tongue! Me modda say dat tongue so sharp you could fillet a bolo-fish[1] wid it. When she get me alone, Fatima tell me: "Picken of Susu woman no good." She say I bad. "Casilla go com 'cross de water for you when de night black an' no moon in de sky." She frighten me. Fadda say we must be kind to her - she don loss two picken to de fever when de rains don com, now she barren woman. But I no de lek um!

De first wife, Okrafa, she bigger dan me fadda. She get plenty picken wid um. She always laughin' an' jokin'. She gib me good chop when I go visit; sometime she gib me pig trotter, I de lek too much. Ev'rybody love her, dem say she wise woman. When she look me in de eye, I t'ink say she see ev'ry blessed t'ing in there. When she cottin' fish wid de big cleaver, I am glad I'm not dat fish. When she dance to de drom beat, ev'rybody want dance wid her.

***

Ma Conteh, she deh[2] odder side de village. I must cross de beach for dem beer. She get a big fridge dat woman, never we see one here before dis time. Dey puttin' in kerosene lek in we own lamp, but I no sabbe how dat liquid make de cold in de one an' de light in de odder. Dat a pow'ful magic dat! Me fadda him say: "Sardine pay for de fridge. Dem Fante men dem de lek cold beer too moch!" Me, I t'inkin' "What about mi fadda?"

---

1. skate
2. lives

I de lek dis time. Dry season don come, him bring small wind. I can hear him whisperin' in de palm. Him make de water dance an' de fish swim close to de land. Wah! You hear dat? Coconut done drop to de sand! What happen if dat bin fall on me head? Dey say it can kill a man. Better it fall on Mr Ibrahim! I go cot um for de milk. It's a hard work dat. I must cot off de flesh wid me cotlass. I give pow'ful blow, lek me fadda don show me. Dat's a good one! De milk run cool down me t'roat. No com out Ma Conteh fridge dat one! Allah be praise for dat.

When I leavin' de palm shade, de sand hot too much. I must jost ron to de water. Look at dem crab scatt'rin', dem ronnin' lek de wind, never I catch one. Always dey fly down dem black hole onder de sand. If you wait, dey com out slow slow. First is comin' de eyes - *on sticks!* Den is comin' de body, same, same colour lek de sand. Dey always watchin', always ready to ron. Now me feet is in de water; dat feel good! I follow de line where de waves is breakin', ronnin' away when de big one com, lek dem small bird dat com here after de rains don don. Look dat Kroo man on de water yonder. Dem Kroo, dem lazy pass all! He lyin' in dat canoe, I de see um when de water lift um op, den I no de see um. There he is again, hat cov'rin' de face. Look de arms an' legs danglin' over de side. There is a fishin' line in each one. What him go do if four fish bite togedder? I tink say he go wake op quick time!

"What you lookin' at, Momadu?"

"Eh, Kwame, you make me jomp!" Dat me fren. Him a Fante boy, same age lek meself. He been gon long time. "When you don com back?"

"Jost I com. Sardine is ronnin', tomorrow we go fish Turtle Islands. Why you no com wid os?"

"Eh, Fante man, you no get school?"

"What use school for fish'man? Dey teach you catch bonga? Dey teach you catch sardine?"

"Dey no teach me not'ing. Bot Mr Ibrahim him beat me plenty if I no go. Me modda she go vex wid me, maybe Casilla com for me dis time."

"Wah, Temne boy, you frighten too moch. Who dat Casilla anyway?"

"You no sabbe Casilla? You no hear of dat white devil? He cross de water, take we black people in de night when we no get moon. Dem people *never* com back again."

"Dat an ole titty tale! We get dat same devil, we call um Kumdumbwe, bot no one believe dat no more. Anyway you no get eyes in you' head - you no see de moon las' night?"

"Never mind de moon las' night, what if cloud cover him? Casilla him see ev'ryt'ing, him wait his time."

"Momadu, you get a big imagination. I sabbe fine you want com. I see it in you' eyes. I go com for you before son op. If Casilla com, him take we both!"

MARTIN WALSH

Highwayman

Imagine this: you've had a few
then wander in the shadows,
a mile of street and neon light,
the smell of Friday atmosphere,
perfume, smoke and clubs;
the nose in crucifixion
and the curry houses cruel.

At the hole in the wall a voice,
above the bleep of your pin number.
However, it's a different kind
of hunger, rasping at your ear,
an edge within a sheath of high,
a stink of pure intent.

Crossing swords with hit and run
or silently deliver, your fist
of notes is like an autocue.

DOUGLAS W. GRAY

Labelled

Instead of this: a hole in the sleeve
of my shirt, worn and dirty shoes,
a torn leather jacket from the sales;
mohair patches stippled round my chin.

The state I'm in, and work is much to blame.
So how about some RayBans for tomorrow,
the outlook smelling pretty, where I can be
a million bucks, a magnet for the girls?

Famous names are rubbing at my shoulders:
Ben Sherman, Calvin Klein, Giorgio Armani;
the world upon my shoulders would be mine.
But mes amis, poetry just isn't worth a Fcuk.
So what do you do? Exactly.

DOUGLAS W. GRAY

30 second wonder

skirt wrenched
up, tights torn
wrists pinned
back in fake arrest

belt yanked
loose, zip ripped
ankles bound
by denim cuffs

a hoarse bark:
Platinum-Blonde
goes down
on Ginger Freckles

dry-mouthed
she wipes her face
takes the tenner
taunts

his stuttered shame
turns her heels
and sways back
to her patch

April 2006

PAULINA VANDERBILT

High Beltaine: rites of passage

The left fist slams the mouth
stunting the shy rejection
as the fire light writhes
in the clearing
in the clearing tonight

The right milks the breast
kneading budding rises
as desires rage higher
in the clearing
out of hearing tonight

The knees steer hips
prizing lips dry
despite ravenous rites
in the clearing
no veering tonight

The blade slices the seal
branding in blood-tainted semen
Man's divine rights
in the clearing
on the shearling tonight

Like a sigh she slips the Escort
wiping her viscid thighs
while the fires die
In the clearing
Disappearing tonight

PAULINA VANDERBILT

The Truth About Harry

The trick was to keep the new minaret on your right and always follow the downward sloping streets. Following this rule, eventually Marie emerged on Fountain Square, its entrance blocked by drifts of taxis dropping off or picking up.

Winter was coming and, though there were peaches on the trees (real peaches you could eat), it was almost time to go home. Her husband, Harry, would stay on. He would come back to Falkirk for the Christmas break, return here after Hogmanay. All the men in Harry's office agreed with him that winters in Baku were cold and bleak. They pointed east across the Caspian – "The Steppe," they said. The guidebooks described the climate as mild. Marie chose to believe Harry.

In Fountain Square the local men sat among the acacia trees, gossiping or watching people pass. In shirtsleeves and pale slacks, they played chess or backgammon, smoked pungent cigarettes and fretted thick black beads. Marie, her shopper on her arm, sailed out into the space, picking up images and scents and sounds and anecdotes, a gesture here, a shrug or grimace there, a snap of triumph – Knight to Queen 4 – Checkmate.

"Hello. Mrs Sullivan?" the girl said.

Marie glanced down at the hand laid on her arm then back to the girl. A sweet face. Twenty (though she might be seventeen). Brown eyes accentuated with dark pencil. The girl's perfect lips were drawn into a smile on bowstrings of affection. Recognition clicked.

"I'm Nara," the girl said.

"Yes," Marie said. "We met at the Irish Bar. You were playing pool."

"With Harry and Bob." Nara laughed.

She was a sweet thing. Marie recalled her giggling a lot.

"How are you?" Marie asked.

"It is a beautiful day," Nara said.

"Yes."

"Mrs Sullivan."

"Marie," the older woman said.

"Marie," Nara said, looking directly at her. She did have beautiful eyes. "I wanted you to know that Harry will be taken care of. His washing and his ironing will be done and I will make sure he eats twice a day, good food and not too much alcohol."

"Really?" Marie said. "That's not necessary. He's lived alone before."

Nara smiled and nodded. "You seemed so nice, I didn't want you to worry."

"Thank you," Marie said.

Nara said, "You are very welcome."

"Well. Goodbye," Marie said.

"Until next year." Nara held out a slim, soft hand with long painted nails. Marie took the hand. It was a lovely hand.

"Yes," she said.

They parted. Marie continued down towards the end of the square and the grander streets near the sea front. She paused once and glanced back. The girl was still heading uphill, threading through the crowd in the autumn sunshine. Her slim figure seemed weightless.

"So," Marie said. She sighed, realising she too felt a momentary lightness. Yes. A weight had been lifted from her. It was a burden of which Marie had been quite unaware ten minutes earlier. She felt extremely satisfied.

JOHN BOLLAND

Dream Sequence

The ferry south was escorted by mermaids.
Round her prow, their stormy indigo hair
darkened the water; now and again, their scales
would glitter at us out of the waves.

But once we got into the shallows I saw,
quite clearly, they were fakes.
Those fish-tails all showed definite wear and tear,
and beneath they were decent in
Marks & Spencers' knickers: I glimpsed the design; just like my own.

I was only a little dismayed. On landing, I gave
the tall dark handsome man who kept the hotel
three titanium apples – a three-night stay –
from my sewing-basket, and climbed his stair.

On every door in the place, tiny daguerrotypes showed
the women who'd been. In Room 1-5
I turned the elaborate bedcover down. It was hiding
three Benares brassware apples.
                              If spells were true
then he and I were now at one another's mercy.

That remained to be seen: I
reminded myself this man was regional manager
for the mermaids,

and I dressed for dinner with care.

JUDITH TAYLOR

Transient

Travel made easy: I can be leaving Liverpool
and never have breathed its air.

Approaching, tilted, we caught a windowful of dark red roofs
and a brown, meandering river – nothing I recognised –

then touchdown. Now we're pretty well sealed
for the time we pass on the tarmac,

and I look at a book:
there's nothing I need to see, here.

It's later, tilting again, I'll watch
for the dark red fields and the looping river I know –

Strathmore. For a road or two I remember;
for a town.

And we were incomers there,
never left to forget it. Still,

it's all there is I could call home, if I had to.
And I find I look – from the car, the train, the plane –

whenever I skirt around it.

Liverpool, where the mail from everywhere passes through:
we are taxiing out. The sudden leap in speed,

pushing against us, and the leap
away from contact, leaving the ground.

I always count to that moment.
Free, gone. Unstoppable now.

Beside me, you look out,
hoping for one more glimpse of the Runcorn Bridge: you tell me

it's the only sight of the old place you remember.

JUDITH TAYLOR

Wakeful

I can't sleep
until everything is quiet.

Till the last party of girls comes screeching,
kitten-heeled,
home.
        Till all the late-night music's played away,
and the last seduction attempt has petered out
in a queasy stupor.

Till the lonely PlayStation games are all abandoned;
till the final cat
has finished dragging the rubbish;

till the babies have been cried to sleep
everywhere, and the mobiles over their cots
are settled down to rest.

Till the fathers have come in
– car-doors slammed, footfalls slurring
over gravel to reach the door
                        (but not the police,
not this time, with something terrible) –

and the shouting has begun,
gone on
and on till it's just past bearable

and has ended,
and there's nothing more.
Till the whole house is silent and the last child
turns over; closes her eyes

closes them tight
to wait for morning.

JUDITH TAYLOR

Author biographies

RICHARD L. ANDERSON was born in Ayrshire and lived in several other parts of Scotland before settling in Aberdeenshire in 1975. He worked in Aberdeen and Aberdeenshire as a surveyor then retired and took up creative writing in 2000. His poetry often comments on life in Scottish small towns.

JOHN BOLLAND writes novels, short fiction and poetry. Raised in Paisley, he has lived and worked in Aberdeenshire for 17 years. His short fiction and poetry has been published by *Pulp.Net*, *The Glasgow Seeker* and in the *Snacks After Swimming* anthology. He is currently working on his 3rd novel.

MICHEL DUDROPT was born in France and worked in West Africa as a photographer, then moved to Scotland and worked offshore. He now lives in Aberdeen writing plays, short stories and scripts.

DOUGLAS W. GRAY lives in Aberdeen, and is a founder member of the Dead Good Poets, a 'reading for charity' poetry group. He is published widely in the small press scene, and has edited poetry magazines. Awards include: first prize in the *Féile Filíochta International Poetry Competition 2001*, and most recently, first prize in the *Ayr800 Open Poetry Competition 2005*. He is also a publisher of poetry chapbooks and runs Koo Press.

REBECCA JONES is a poet and geologist now living in Australia. Her poetry has appeared in print, and in 2001 she took an acting role in *Soul Traders*, a collaboration between Lemon Tree Writers and Spotlight Theatre.

ELAINE KAY: I grew up in Paisley, then moved to Aberdeen. I have been writing poetry and short stories for nearly half my life now, and joined Lemon Tree Writers in 2002. My poetry has been published in *Pushing Out the Boat* and *Meeting Points*.

ROBERT MCKAY LOTHIAN has been a member of Lemon Tree Writers since 2002 and has had poetry published in *Storm* and *Pushing out the Boat*. His stories often feature surreal or magical elements and his own quirky sense of humour.

OLIVIA MCMAHON, born in England of Irish parents, has lived for nearly 40 years now in Scotland. She writes novels, novellas and EFL text books and is also widely published as a poet, including *Domestic Verses* (Koo Press). She was a founder member of the Lemon Tree Writers.

IAN MORRISON was born and has lived and worked in the North East all his life. He has had a number of short stories, prose extracts and poems published previously, including in *New Writing Scotland*, *Pushing Out the Boat*, etc. A novel is currently making very slow progress.

AIDAN MULKERRIN, whose interests range across history, modern novels, film and travel, lives in Aberdeen, and is working on a novel of his own.

ANN NICOL has been interested in writing for many years, particularly in the Doric. As a retired legal secretary, she finds time to write and is assisted in her efforts by the Lemon Tree Writers Group in Aberdeen.

MARIANNE NICOLL: I work for Angus Council, supporting adults improving their literacy, communication and numeracy skills. I have always enjoyed the visual arts, countryside and words. Solitary walks mirror moods.

MARK PITHIE is inspired by Aberdeen and all the images it conjures up. He is published in various places and came 3rd in Ottakers Poetry Competition in 2001 with his poem "Linda Bailey". He is currently thinking about his first collection.

STEVE PORTER: Inverness-born writer who lives in Spain. Author of *The Iberian Horseshoe – A Journey*, chapters of which can be read online at www.badosa.com. Poems published online by www.laurahird.com. Other poems have appears in *Cutting Teeth*, *Northwords* and *Orbis*.

ROBERT RAMSAY is a farmer and countryman who came late to writing, mostly poetry, taking his inspiration from the rural landscape, usually Angus, and the spirit and character of the people who inhabit those places.

In four years' attendance at LTW, **HELEN ELIZABETH RAMSEY** has been on time twice. She'd *like* this scatty infamy to be overshadowed by originality, wit and style, but in the meantime keeps a hopeful pen in her bag. Hopeful, that is, that the lid stays on and ink doesn't stain the lining.

GRÁINNE SMITH used to dream of writing fulltime... now she does! To see what she writes and otherwise gets up to, visit www.grainnesmith.co.uk.

JOSÉ SOLERA, a Spaniard, lived in Aberdeen from 2002-05 during which time he became involved with LTW activities. He owes a great deal to his fellow Lemon Tree writers, or 'limonistas', as friend M. Walsh nicknames the group. He hopes there will be plenty times when he might be found around in town again.

JUDITH TAYLOR is from Perthshire originally, now living in Aberdeen. Her poetry has appeared in a number of magazines and in the Lemon Tree collection *Meeting Points*, and her chapbook *Earthlight* was published earlier this year by Koo Press.

KNOTBROOK TAYLOR: I never know what is going to trigger the next poem: it could be a dream, a feeling or a phrase: whatever it is, poetry is something I need to do to keep a creative dimension to my life. The Lemon Tree Writers has really helped me develop.

PAULINA VANDERBILT writes fiction for children and poetry. For inspiration she observes her own children and the teenagers she teaches. Good stories are all around us; the secret is to open up to them and craft them until they sparkle like your finest silver. Paulina has been published in the *Lemon Tree brochure*, *Pushing Out the Boat*, and the Lemon Tree Publication *Meeting Points*.

CAL WALLACE writes short stories, each of which he strives to approach from an unusual angle. He regards each story as an experiment, and as part of the training process for his yet-to-be-written novel. When he grows up he's going to be a spaceman.

MARTIN WALSH a marine biologist, turned to tennis and writing fiction later in life. Although the top-spin backhand remains elusive, he is now published and this year read from one of his African stories on Radio 4.

CATRIONA YULE started writing poetry in the early 90s and also writes fiction and drama. Her play *Kitten Heels* was given a semi-staged production at Aberdeen Arts Centre in 2005 and she is currently developing her fiction writing through the Storylines course in the Open College of the Arts programme. She performs with the Blue Salt Collective.